READER'S DELIGHT

Biography of
Dr. B.R. Ambedkar

READER'S DELIGHT

AN IMPRINT OF RAMESH PUBLISHING HOUSE

NEW DELHI

ISBN 978-93-5012-252-5
HSN Code : 49011010

Published by: Alok Kumar Gupta *for* Reader's Delight
(An Imprint of Ramesh Publishing House)

Admin. Office: 12-H, New Daryaganj Road, Opp. Officers' Mess,
New Delhi-110002 ① 23261567, 23275224, 23275124

Showroom: ● Balaji Market, Nai Sarak, Delhi-6 ① 23253720, 23282525
● 4457, Nai Sarak, Delhi-6 ① 23918938

E-Mail: info@rameshpublishinghouse.com
Website: www.rameshpublishinghouse.com

PREFACE

Dr. Bhimrao Ambedkar was an Indian jurist, scholar, political leader and a Buddhist revivalist. He was the Chief Architect of the Indian Constitution. He played a great role in framing of Indian Constitution. He was the first Law Minister of India. He spent his whole life fighting against Social discrimination and untouchability. He was posthumously awarded the highest civilian award—the Bharat Ratna, in 1990.

Dr. Ambedkar is viewed as messiah of dalits and downtrodden in India. Though he was the son of large family of then called 'Untouchable' Mahar caste, still he managed to get the highest degree of education and scaled even higher political heights and wisdom.

The inside pages contain an interesting and elevating account of how an average boy of a low-caste and not so rich family fought against the discrimination and became the messiah of dalits and downtrodden in India. The book also gives its readers minute detail about his life and personality. We hope the book will prove successful in clinching the readers' interest.

— **Publisher**

CONTENTS

INTRODUCTION

Dr Bhimrao Ambedkar, popularly known as Babasaheb Ambedkar, was the Chief architect of the Indian Constitution. He was a well-known politician and an eminent jurist. His efforts to eradicate the social evils like untouchablity and caste restrictions were remarkable. He, throughout his life, fought for the rights of the dalits and other socially backward classes. He was appointed as the nation's first Law Minister in the Cabinet of Jawaharlal Nehru. He was posthumously awarded the Bharat Ratna, India's highest civilian honour, in 1990.

Bhimrao was a victim of caste discrimination. His parents hailed from the Hindu Mahar caste, which was then viewed as 'untouchable' by the upper class. Due to this, he had to face severe discriminations from every corner of the society. The discrimination and humiliation haunted him even at the Army school, run by British government. Discrimination followed wherever he went. In 1908, he got the opportunity to study at the Elphinstone College, Bombay. Besides clearing all the exams successfully he also obtained a scholarship from the Gayakwad ruler of Baroda, Sayaji Rao III. He graduated from the Bombay University in 1912 with Political Science and Economics subjects. He was sponsored by Sayaji Rao to go for higher studies in America and England.

After returning from there, he was appointed as the Defence secretary to the King of Baroda. Even, there also he had to face the humiliation for being an 'Untouchable'. With the help of the former Bombay Governor Lord Sydenham, he obtained the job of a professor of political economy at the Sydenham College of Commerce and Economics in Bombay. In order to continue his further studies, in 1920, he went to England again on his own expenses. There he was awarded honour of D.Sc by the London University. He also spent few months at the University of Bonn, Germany, to study Economics. On 8 June, 1927, he was awarded a Doctorate by the University of Columbia.

After coming back to India, Dr. Bhimrao Ambedkar decided to fight against the caste discrimination that almost fragmented the nation. Ambedkar opined that there should be separate electoral system for the untouchables and lower caste people. He also favoured the concept of providing reservations for Dalits and other religious communities.

Dr. Ambedkar objected to the decision of Congress and Mahatma Gandhi to call the untouchable community as

Dr.Ambedkar Chairman, Drafting Committee of Indian Constitution with other members

Harijans. He said that even the members of untouchable community were same as the other members of the society. Ambedkar was appointed on the Defence Advisory Committee and the Viceroy's Executive Council as Minister for Labour. His reputation as a scholar led to his appointment as free India's first Law Minister and Chairman of the committee responsible to draft a constitution.

Dr. Bhimrao Ambedkar was appointed as the chairman of the constitution drafting committee. He was also a noted scholar and eminent jurist. Ambedkar emphasized on the construction of a virtual bridge between the classes of the society. According to him, it would be difficult to maintain the unity of the country if the difference among the classes were not met.

Dr. Ambedkar traveled to Sri Lanka in 1950 to attend a convention of Buddhist scholars and monks. After his return, he decided to write a book on Buddhism and soon, converted himself to Buddhism. In his speeches, Ambedkar lambasted the Hindu rituals and caste division. In 1955

Ambedkar founded the "Bharatiya Bauddha Mahasabha". His book *"The Buddha and His Dhamma"* was published posthumously.

Dr. Ambedkar died at his home in Delhi on 6 December, 1956.

He was the greatest sons of India. He experienced the suffering and the cruelty, overcame and awakened millions of India's oppressed to their human rights and stand on an equal footing.

His role in forming modern India through its constitution is immensely laudable.

THE FAMILY HISTORY

Dr. Bhimrao Ambedkar was born on April 14, 1891 to Bhimabai and Ramji Maloji Sakpal Ambavedekar. His father Ramji was an army Subedar posted at Mhow in Madhya Pradesh who had risen to the highest rank an Indian was allowed to hold at that time under British rule. His grandfather also served in British Army. They belonged to the so called 'untouchable' Mahar

Subedar Ramji
father of
Dr. Bhimrao Ambedkar

Hindu lower caste. Bhimabai decided to call her son Bhimrao. His parents already had thirteen children. Despite that, they resolved to make every effort to get him a good education.

Ramji followed the teachings of saint Kabir who taught that devotion to God alone is important. Ramji did not believe in difference of caste, creed and religion. It was his belief that all who performed 'Hari Bhajan' (Prayer) belonged to God.

— ✱✱✱ —

CHILDHOOD AND EARLY EDUCATION

While Bhimrao was at the age of six, his mother died. The family was brought up by Ramji's sister Meerabai until Ramji married a widow named Jijabai. Ramji was a strict, pious man. He was a vegetarian and teetotaller. He used to read stories from the epics 'Mahabharata' and 'Ramayana' to his children, and sang devotional songs to them. In this way, home life was still happy for Bhimrao and his brothers and sisters. He never forgot the influence of his father who taught him about the rich cultural tradition shared by all Indians.

Ramji retired from the army after 14 years of service at the rank of Subedar-Major of the 2nd Grenadiers. The family moved to Dapoli in Konkan and then to Satara. Bhimrao and elder brother, Anand, were enrolled in the cantonment Government High School.

Bhimrao was an average student. While studying in Satara, many of his classmates left for good jobs in Bombay. He too wanted to go to Bombay and get a job and become independent. He needed money for the railway fare. For three days, he tried to steal his aunt's purse and at last when he got it, he found just half anna (three paise) in it. He was ashamed of his deed. He realized that if he ever were to be successful, he would have to concentrate more on his studies and do it on his own. He, then became interested in studies. He studied not just the prescribed books in school but any book he came across. His father was too pleased when he digressed from school books but he never said 'no' whenever Bhimrao wanted a book. He even borrowed money to quench his thirst of books.

A broad-minded Brahmin teacher admired Bhimrao's lively mind. His family name was Ambedkar. The teacher liked Bhimrao so much that he changed Bhimrao's surname from Ambavadekar to Ambedkar.

Soon he was winning the highest praise and admiration from all his teachers. They urged Ramji to get the best education for his son Bhimrao. So Ramji and his family moved to Bombay. The family found a house in a locality where the poorest of the poor lived. There was just one room for the entire family. This was at once the kitchen, the bedroom and the study. There was not space enough even for two to sleep. Bhimrao would go to bed early. Near his head there was a grinding stone and at his feet a goat. The father would be awake till two in the night. He would then lie down. The boy would get up, light the kerosene lamp without a chimney and begin to study.

Bhimrao studied at the Elphinstone High School in Bombay. Even there, one of his teachers constantly mocked him, saying that of what use was an educated Mahar. In the big city, where life was more modern than in the villages, Bhimrao found that he was still called an 'untouchable' and treated as if something made him different and bad even at his famous school.

One day, the teacher called him up to the blackboard to do a sum. All the other boys jumped up and made a big fuss. Their lunch boxes were stacked behind the blackboard as they believed that Bhimrao would pollute the food. When he wanted to learn Sanskrit, the language of the Hindu holy scriptures, he was told that it was forbidden for 'untouchables' to do so. He had to study Persian instead but he taught himself Sanskrit later in life.

Bhimrao swallowed these insults and controlled his anger. He passed his matriculation examination in 1907. The Mahar community felicitated him on his achievement on becoming one of the first persons of untouchable origin to enter a college in India. This success provoked celebrations in his community and in a public ceremony he was presented a biography of Buddha by his teacher.

— ✳✳✳ —

MARRIAGE

Bhimrao passed his Matriculation examination in 1907. He was then seventeen years old. The same year his marriage with Ramabai was commenced. Their marriage took place in a shed in Byculla Market, Bombay as per Hindu

Dr. Ambedkar with Dr. Sharada Kabir

customs. In those days, the marriages were arranged in quite young age. While Bhimrao was seventeen, his wife was just nine years old. However, he continued his studies as usual after his marriage. Ramabai gave birth to her first son, Yashwant in the same year.

Later, on 15 April, 1948 many years after the death of Ramabai in 1935, he married a Saraswatha Brahmin lady – Dr. Sharda Kabir; she was working in the same hospital at Bombay where he was treated for sometime.

— ✳✳✳ —

THE IMPACT OF UNTOUCHABILITY

Early in his life Bhimrao began to taste the bitter reality of being born an 'untouchable', he noticed that he and his family were treated differently. At high school he had to sit in the corner of the room on a rough mat, away from the desks of the other students. At break-time, he was not allowed to drink water using the cups his fellow school children used. He had to hold his cupped hands out to have water poured into them by the school watchman. Once, provoked by an uncontrollable fit of thirst, he drank water from the public reservoir. He was caught and beaten by the higher caste Hindus. These experiences were deeply etched onto his mind. He realized the very plight of anyone born 'untouchable'. Teachers never touched his notebooks. Bhim did not know why he should be treated differently—what was wrong with him?

Once, to spend their summer holidays, he and his elder brother had to travel to Goregaon, where their father worked as a cashier. They got off the train and waited for a long time at the station, but Ramji could not arrive to meet them. The station master seemed kind, and asked them who they were and where they were going. The boys were very well-dressed, clean, and polite. Bhimrao, without thinking, told him they were Mahars. The station master was stunned–his face instantly changed its kindly expression and he hurriedly went away from there.

They decided to hire a bullock-cart to take them to their father–this was before motor cars were used as taxis–but the cartmen had heard that the boys were 'untouchables', and wanted nothing to do with them. Finally, they had to pay double the usual fare of the journey, and they drove the cart themselves, while the cartman walked beside it. He was afraid of being polluted by the boys, because they were 'untouchables'. However, the extra money offered persuaded him that he could have his cart 'purified' later! Throughout the journey, Bhimrao thought constantly about what had happened—yet he could not understand the reason for it. He and his brother were clean and neatly dressed. Yet they were supposed to pollute and make unclean everything they touched and all that touched them. He could not understand the reason as he was a child then.

Bhimrao never forgot this incident. As he grew up, many such senseless insults made him realise that what Hindu society called 'untouchability' was something stupid, cruel, and unreasonable. His sister had to cut his hair at home because the village barbers were afraid of being polluted by an 'untouchable'. If he asked her why they were 'untouchables', she could only answer—"that is the way it has always been"; Bhimrao could not be satisfied with this answer. He knew that — "it has always been that way" does not mean that there is a just reason for it—or that it had to stay that way forever. It could be changed.

Bhimrao had to face insults many times during his student life and during service in India as well. There were many such episodes which made a deep impact on his mind. One such episode is described in detail under the topic "The Baroda Nightmare" in the coming pages of this book.

However, during his stints in America and London, he never faced any such discriminating incident.

— *** —

HIGHER STUDIES

Bhimrao joined the Elphinstone College for further education. After completing his Intermediate course, he received a scholarship from the Maharaja of Baroda, Sayaji Rao, and attained a Bachelors in Arts in 1912. His father and mentor, Ramji died in Bombay in February, 1912.

Sayaji Rao, the Maharaja of Baroda had a scheme to send a few outstanding scholars abroad for further studies. For it, Bhimrao was selected– but he had to sign an agreement to serve Baroda State for ten years on finishing his studies.

He went to the USA in July, 1913 where he studied at the world-famous Columbia University, New York. The freedom and equality he experienced in America made a very deep impact on Bhimrao. It was really refreshing for him to be able to live a normal life, free from the caste prejudice of India. He could do anything he pleased— but he devoted all his time in studying. He studied eighteen hours a day. Visits to bookshops was his favourite pastime.

Economics and Sociology were his main subjects. Within just two years, he was awarded a degree in Master of Arts and the following year he attained Doctorate in Philosophy from Columbia University in 1916. Then he left Columbia and went to England, where he joined the London School of Economics to study Economics and Political Science. However, he had to leave London in June 1917, before completing his studies because the scholarship granted by the State of Baroda had expired. He was given permission to return and submit his thesis within four years. He sent his precious and much loved collection of books back on a steamer, but it was unfortunately torpedoed and sunk by a German submarine. Bhimrao had to wait three more years before he could return to London to complete his studies.

— *** —

THE BARODA NIGHTMARE

Bhimrao returned to India to take up a high post in Baroda as agreed. He was given good job in the Baroda Civil Service. Bhimrao now had a doctorate, and was holding a top job. Yet, he again ran into the worst features of the Hindu caste system. This was all the more painful, because for the past four years he had been abroad, living free from the label of 'untouchable.'

No one came to welcome him when he reached Baroda. Worse still, even the peons at the office where he worked would not hand over files and papers to him—they just threw them onto his desk. Nor would they give him water to drink. No respect was given to him, merely because of his caste. He could not get a house to live in. Even though he complained to the authorities, it was useless. Even non-Hindus did not treat him properly.

He had to go from hotel to hotel looking for a room, but none of them would take him in. At last he had found a place to live in a Parsi guest house, but only because he had finally decided to keep his caste secret.

He lived there in very uncomfortable conditions, in a small bedroom with a tiny bathroom attached. He was totally alone there with no one to talk to. There were no electric lights or even oil lamps—so the place was completely dark at night.

Ambedkar was hoping to find somewhere else to live through his civil service job, but before he could, one morning as he was leaving for office, a dozen of angry Parsi men carrying sticks arrived outside his room. They accused him of polluting the hotel and warned him to get out by evening – or else...! What could he do? He could not stay with either of the two acquaintances he had in Baroda for the same reason—his low caste. Bhimrao felt totally miserable and dejected. He had no choice but to leave.

In Ambedkar's words, "That scene of dozen Parsis armed with sticks line before me in a menacing mood, and myself standing before them with a terrified look imploring for mercy, is a scene which so long a period as eighteen years had not succeeded in fading away. I can even vividly recall it—and I never recall it without tears in my eyes. It was then for the first time that I learnt that a person who is an untouchable to a Hindu is also an untouchable to a Parsi."

After only eleven days in his new job, he had to part with and return to Bombay. There, he tried to find ways to make a living for his growing family. He worked as a private tutor, as an accountant and even tried to start a small business there, advising people about investments but it too failed once customers learned of his caste.

Somehow in 1918, he became professor of Political Economy at Sydenham College in Bombay. There, his students recognised him as a brilliant teacher and scholar. Even though he was successful with students, other professors objected to his sharing the same drinking water jug they all used for them.

Dr. Ambedkar carried on this job and saved some money to return to London to complete his studies.

— *** —

RISING AS LEADER OF UNTOUCHABLES

Dr. Ambedkar, somehow, was able to return to London in 1920 to complete his studies in Economics at London School of Economics. He also enrolled to study as a Barrister at Gray's Inn. In 1923, he returned to India with a Doctorate in Economics from the London School of Economics. He was perhaps the first Indian to have a Doctorate from this world-famous institution. He had also qualified as a Barrister-at-Law.

He knew that back in India, nothing had changed. His qualifications meant nothing as far as the practice of untouchability was concerned—it was still an obstacle in his career. However, he had received the best education anyone in the world could get, and was well equipped to be a leader of his community. He could argue with and persuade the best minds of his time on equal terms. He was an expert on the law, and could give convincing evidence before British commissions as an eloquent and gifted speaker. He dedicated the rest of his life to fight against injustice caused by untouchability.

Dr. Ambedkar became known by his increasing number of followers – those 'untouchables' he urged to awake as

Babasaheb Ambedkar. In July 1924, knowing the great value and importance of education, he founded an association called "Bahiskrit Hitakarini Sabha". The aim of the Sabha was to uplift the downtrodden socially and politically and bring them to the level of the others in the Indian Society. The Sabha aimed at scrapping the caste system from the Hindu religion. The Sabha started free schools for the young and the old and set up hostels, reading rooms, and free libraries. To improve the lives of untouchables, education had to reach everyone and opportunities had to be provided at grass roots level. Dr. Ambedkar took the grievances of the untouchables to court and got them justice. Soon he became a father-figure to the poor and downtrodden.

On March 19-20, 1927 a conference of the depressed classes was held at Mahad. Ten thousand delegates, workers and leaders attended it. Ambedkar condemned the British for banning the recruitment of 'untouchables' into the military. He declared, "No lasting progress can achieved unless we put ourselves through a threefold process of purification. We must improve the general tone of our demeanour, re-tone our pronunciation and revitalize our thoughts. I, therefore, ask you now to take a vow to renounce eating carrion, the ... flesh of ... animals, from this moment. ...Make an unflinching resolve not to eat the thrown away crumbs. It is time we rooted out of our minds the ideas of high and low. We will attain self-elevation only if we learn self-help, regain our self-respect and gain self-knowledge."

Ambedkar, due to his experience of the humiliation and injustice of untouchability, knew that justice would not be granted by others. Those who suffer injustice must secure justice for themselves.

The first Satyagraha at Mahad against the prohibition on untouchables to have drinking water at the public pond. (25.12.1927)

The Bombay Legislature had already passed a Bill allowing everyone to use public water tanks and wells.

Mahad Municipality had thrown open the local water tank four years earlier, but untill then not even one 'untouchable' had dared to drink or draw water from that. In 1927, he led a procession from the Conference on a peaceful demonstration to the Chavdar Tank. He knelt and drank water from it. After he set this example, thousands of others felt courageous enough to follow him. They drank water from the tank and made history. For hundreds of years, 'untouchables' had been forbidden from drinking water from public water tanks and wells.

When some upper caste people saw them drinking water, they believed the tank had been polluted and violently attacked them, but he insisted that violence would not help. He had given his word that they would agitate peacefully.

The upper cast people beat the delegates, pulled down the conference pulpit, threw away all the cooked food and broke all the vessels. Ambedkar told his followers to stay calm and not to retaliate. Later the other people performed rituals to 'purify' the 'defiled' water. Ambedkar then vowed to offer a satyagraha and re-establish his people's right to share the water tank.

On December 25, 1927 thousands responded to Ambedkar's call. Speaker after speaker spoke, passions rose and the vast gathering waited for the satyagraha to begin with intense anticipation. The satyagraha was deferred when the matter was referred to the court. At the end of conference, a copy of the *Manusmruti*, the age-old code of the Hindus that gave rise to the caste system, was ceremoniously burnt. In a thundering voice, Ambedkar demanded in its place a new *Smruti*, devoid of all social stratification. This act sent shockwaves through the nation.

Ambedkar started a Marathi journal *Bahishkrit Bharat* (The Excluded of India). Through this, he urged his people to start non-violent agitation to secure the right of entry to the Kala Ram Temple at Nasik. 'Untouchables' had always been forbidden to enter Hindu temples. The demonstration lasted for a month. Then they were told they would be able to take part in the annual temple festival. However, at the festival they had stones thrown at them and were not allowed to take part. Courageously, they resumed their peaceful agitation. The temple remained closed for about a year, as its entrance was blocked by them. The matter was later decided by court in an impartial manner.

— ✳✳✳ —

ROUND TABLE CONFERENCE

On the other side, the Indian Freedom Movement had gained momentum under the leadership of Mahatma Gandhi. In 1929, Ambedkar made the controversial decision to co-operate with the all-British Simon Commission which was to look into setting up a responsible Indian Government of India. The Congress decided to boycott the Commission and drafted its own version of a constitution for free India. Unfortunately the Congress version made no provisions for the depressed classes. Ambedkar became more skeptical of the Congress' commitment to safeguard the rights of the depressed classes. Considering his influence and concern for the depressed classes he was invited to the Round Table Conference in London, held from November 1930 to January 1931, to represent the depressed classes. He emphatically declared there that before the British came to India the evil of 'untouchability' was rampant and even after 150 years of British rule, the evil had not abated. The British had done nothing to alleviate the status of the depressed classes.

In Ambedkar's words, "The Depressed Classes of India also join in the demand for replacing the British Government by a Government of the people and by the people... Our wrongs have remained as open sores and have not been righted although 150 years of British rule have rolled away. Of what good is such a Government to anybody?"

He declared that India must have a minimum of Dominion Status. He pressed for a separate electorate for the depressed classes.

A second conference was held soon, which Mahatma Gandhi attended representing the Congress Party. Ambedkar met Gandhiji in Bombay before they went to London. Gandhiji told him that he had read what Ambedkar said at the first conference. He told Ambedkar he knew him to be a real Indian patriot.

— *** —

THE POONA PACT

At the Second Round Table Conference, Ambedkar asked for a separate electorate for the Depressed Classes. He said, "Hinduism has given us only insults, misery, and humiliation. A separate electorate would mean that the 'untouchables' would vote for their own candidates and be allotted their votes separate from the Hindu majority."

Gandhi fiercely opposed separate electorate for untouchables, though he accepted separate electorate for all other minority groups such as Muslims and Sikhs, saying he feared that separate electorates for untouchables would further divide Hindu community into two groups. However, the British agreed with Ambedkar and announced the Communal Award for separate electorates.

As the news came that separate electorates had been granted Ambedkar was made a hero by thousands of his followers on his return from Bombay—even though he always said that people should not idolise him. Gandhi felt that separate electorates would separate the Harijans from the Hindus. The very thought that the Hindus would be divided, pained him grievously. He started a fast unto death to prevent the communal divide.

Gandhi's fast provoked huge civil unrest across India, and orthodox Hindu leaders, Congress politicians and activists such as Madan Mohan Malaviya and other organized joint meetings with Ambedkar and his supporters at Yervada.

Senior Congress leaders knew that only Ambedkar could save Gandhi's life by withdrawing the demand for separate electorates. They tried their best to persuade him. Initially, he refused, saying it was his duty to do the best he could for his people–no matter what.

Later, fearing a communal reprisal and genocide of untouchables, under massive coercion from the supporters of Gandhi, Ambedkar relented and visited Gandhi, who was at that time in Yervada jail. This agreement, which saw Gandhi end his fast, was called the Poona Pact. As a result of the

Poona Pact Sept. 24, 1932. From the left—Barrister M.R. Jaykar, Sir Tej Bahadur Sapru, Kajolkar, P. Balu and other leaders are seen outside the Yerawada Central Jail.

agreement, Ambedkar dropped the demand for separate electorates that was promised through the British Communal Award prior to Ambedkar's meeting with Gandhi. Instead, a certain number of seats were promised to be reserved specifically for 'Untouchables' or the 'Depressed Class' in the elections.

— *** —

SOME MAJOR EVENTS

On October 13, 1935, at a conference in Nasik, Dr. Ambedkar reviewed the progress made on the condition of the 'untouchables' in the decade since Ambedkar started his agitation. Ambedkar declared that their efforts had not borne the kind of results he had expected. He then made a revolutionary appeal to the 'untouchables'. He encouraged them to forsake the Hindu religion and convert to a religion where they would be treated with equality. The whole nation was shocked.

Dr. Ambedkar being administered the Oath by the first President of Indian Republic Dr. Rajendra Prasad, Jawahar Lal Nehru the then Prime Minister of India, looking on. (1947)

In 1937, the British Government agreed to hold elections on the provincial level. The Congress, Muslim League and Hindu Mahasabha started gearing up for the elections in the Bombay province. On February 17, 1937. Ambedkar and many of his candidates won this with a thumping majority. Around the same time, the Chavdar Taley water dispute which was referred to the Bombay High Court in 1927 finally handed down its verdict in favour of the depressed classes.

Dr. Ambedkar introduced Bills in 1937 to abolish the 'Khoti' system of land tenure in the Konkan region, the serfdom of agricultural tenants and the Mahar "watan" system of working for the Government as slaves. A clause of an agrarian bill referred to the depressed classes as 'Harijans', or people of God. Ambedkar was strongly opposed to this title for the untouchables. He argued that if the 'untouchables' were people of God then all others would be people of monsters. He was against any such reference. But the Indian National Congress succeeded in introducing the term 'Harijan'. Ambedkar felt bitter that they could not have any say in what they were called.

On July 15, 1947, the British Parliament passed the Act of Indian Independence and on August 15, 1947, India became free. The Constituent Assembly of Independent India appointed a Drafting Committee with Dr. Ambedkar as its Chairman to draft the Constitution of India. Dr. Ambedkar was also invited to join the Cabinet as the Minister of Law. Ambedkar toiled over the Constitution while he took care of his ministry. In February 1948, Dr. Ambedkar presented the Draft Constitution before the people of India.

The mammoth effort had taken its toll on Dr. Ambedkar's health. He went to Bombay for treatment and later on recovery, married Dr. Sharada Kabir on April 15, 1948, who worked in the same hospital where he was receiving treatment.

The Constituent Assembly adopted the Draft Constitution as the Constitution of India on November 26, 1949 with all its 356 Articles and eight Schedules and Article 11 which abolished untouchability in all forms.

In October 1948, Dr. Ambedkar submitted the Hindu Code Bill to the Constituent Assembly in an attempt to codify the Hindu law. The Bill caused great divisions even in the Congress party. Consideration for the bill was postponed to September 1951. When the Bill was taken up it was truncated. A dejected Ambedkar relinquished his position as Law Minister from the Cabinet.

— *** —

BOOKS AND RELIGION

Ambedkar was an ardent book lover from the very beginning. While at high school he used to buy books on all subjects which were not even required for his course of study. His father always helped him buy books.

While at America and London, he used to spend most of his time in libraries and bookshops. Infact he sent back a huge collection of books to India which unfortunately sank in the sea with the steamer.

In 1935, Ambedkar was appointed principal of the Government Law College, Mumbai, a position he held for two years. Settling in Mumbai, Ambedkar oversaw the construction of a house, and stocked his personal

Dr. Ambedkar with Professors of Government Law College, Bombay.

library with more than 50,000 books. His wife Ramabai died after a long illness in the same year.

It had been her long-standing wish to go on a pilgrimage to Pandharpur, but Ambedkar had refused to let her go, telling her that he would create a new Pandharpur for her instead of Hinduism's Pandharpur which treated them as untouchables. Speaking at the Yeola Conversion Conference on 13 October, 1935 in Nasik, Ambedkar announced his intention to convert to a different religon and exhorted his followers to leave Hinduism. He later repeated his message at numerous public meetings across India. He later embraced Buddhism along with thousands of his followers.

HIS BOOKS & WORKS

In 1936, Ambedkar founded the Independent Labour Party. He published his book *The Annihilation of Caste* in the same year, based on the thesis he had written in New York. Attaining immense popular success, Ambedkar's work strongly criticized Hindu orthodox religious leaders and the caste system in general. With *'What Congress and Gandhi Have Done to the Untouchables'*, Ambedkar intensified his attacks on Gandhi and the Congress, hypocrisy.

In his work *'Who Were the Shudras?'*, Ambedkar attempted to explain the formation of the Shudras *i.e.*, the lowest caste in hierarchy of Hindu caste system. He also emphasised how Shudras are separate from Untouchables. Ambedkar oversaw the transformation of his political party into the All India Scheduled Castes Federation, although it performed poorly in the elections held in 1946 for the Constituent Assembly of India. In writing a sequel to *'Who Were the Shudras?'* in 1948, Ambedkar lambasted Hinduism in *'The Untouchables'*—A Thesis on the Origins of Untouchability.

— *** —

VIEWS ON PAKISTAN

Dr. Ambedkar published a number of books and pamphlets between 1941 and 1945 including *'Thoughts on Pakistan'*, in which he criticized the Muslim League's demand for a separate Muslim state of Pakistan but considered its concession if Muslims demanded so as expedient.

In this book Ambedkar wrote, "If Muslims truly and deeply desire Pakistan, their choice ought to be accepted". He wrote that if the Muslims are bent on Pakistan, then it must be conceded to them. He asked whether Muslims in the army could be trusted to defend India (then). In the event of Muslims invading India or in the case of a Muslim rebellion, with whom would the Indian Muslims in the army, side? He concluded that, in the interests of the safety of India, Pakistan should be acceded to, should the Muslims demand it. According to Ambedkar, "The Hindu assumption that though Hindus and Muslims were two nations, they could live together under one state, was but an empty sermon, a mad project, to which no sane man would agree."

He was also critical of Islam and its practices in South Asia. While justifying the Partition of India, he condemned the practice of child marriage in Muslim society, as well as the mistreatment of women.

He said, "No words can adequately express the great and many evils of polygamy and concubinage, and especially as a source of misery to a Muslim woman. Take the caste system. Everybody infers that Islam must be free from slavery and caste. While slavery existed, much of its support was derived from Islam and Islamic countries. While the prescriptions by the Prophet regarding the just and humane treatment of slaves contained in the Koran are praiseworthy, there is nothing whatever in Islam that lends support to the abolition of this curse. But if slavery has gone, caste among 'Muslims' has remained."

He wrote that Muslim society is 'even more full of social evils than Hindu Society is' and criticized Muslims for sugarcoating their sectarian caste system with euphemisms like 'brotherhood'. He also criticized the discrimination against the Arzal classes among Muslims who were regarded as 'degraded', as well as the oppression of women in Muslim society through the oppressive purdah system. He alleged that while purdah was also practiced by Hindus, only among Muslims was it sanctioned by religion. He criticized their fanaticism regarding Islam on the grounds that their literalist interpretations of Islamic doctrine made their society very rigid and impermeable to change. He further wrote that Indian Muslims have failed to reform their society unlike Muslims in other countries like Turkey.

— *** —

ARCHITECT OF THE CONSTITUTION

When India gained independence on 15 August 1947, the new Congress-led government invited Dr. Ambedkar to serve as the nation's first Law Minister, which he accepted. On 29 August, 1947, Ambedkar was appointed Chairman of the Constitution Drafting Committee, charged by the Assembly to write India's new Constitution.

The Indian Constitution drafted by Ambedkar has been described as 'first and foremost a social document'. ... 'The majority of India's constitutional provisions are either directly arrived at furthering the aim of social revolution or attempt to foster this revolution by establishing conditions necessary for its achievement.'

Dr. Ambedkar presenting the draft of the Constitution to Dr. Rajendra Prasad, President Constituents Assembly. (Feb. 1948)

The text of the constitution prepared by Ambedkar provided constitutional guarantees and protections for a wide range of civil liberties for individual citizens, including freedom of religion, the abolition of untouchability and the outlawing of all forms of discrimination. Ambedkar argued for extensive economic and social rights for women, and also won the Assembly's support for introducing a system of reservations of jobs in the civil services, schools and colleges for members of scheduled castes and scheduled tribes, a system akin to affirmative action. India's lawmakers hoped to eradicate the socio-economic inequalities and lack of opportunities for India's depressed classes through this measure, which had been originally envisioned as temporary on a need basis. The Constitution was adopted on 26 November 1949 by the Constituent Assembly. It came into force on 26 January, 1950.

Dr. Ambedkar resigned from the cabinet in 1951 following the stalling in parliament of his draft of the Hindu Code Bill, which sought to expound gender equality in the laws of inheritance, marriage and the economy. Although supported by Prime Minister Nehru, the cabinet and many other Congress leaders, it received criticism from a large number of members of parliament.

Ambedkar independently contested an election in 1952 to the lower house of parliament, the Lok Sabha, but was defeated. He was appointed to the upper house of parliament, the Rajya Sabha, in March 1952 and remained a Rajya Sabha member until his death.

— ✳✳✳ —

CONVERSION TO BUDDHISM

Soon after the framing of the Constitution, Ambedkar's mind turned towards Buddha. His mind was thirsting for peace and justice. The bitterness of his mind was ever on the increase. Muslim and Christian missionaries tried hard to attract him and assured equal status in their society. In spite of it, he was not willing to embrace the Christian or the Muslim faith. He attended the Buddhist Conference in Sri Lanka in 1950.

Dr. Ambedkar believed that the Mahar people were an ancient Buddhist community of India who had been forced to live outside villages as outcasts because they refused to renounce their Buddhist practices. He considered this to be—why they became untouchables, and he wrote a book on this topic entitled '*Who were the Shudras?*'

While dedicating a new Buddhist vihara near Pune, Ambedkar announced that he was writing a book on Buddhism, and that as soon as it was finished, he planned to make a formal conversion back to Buddhism. Ambedkar twice visited Burma in 1954; the second time in order to attend the third conference of the World Fellowship of Buddhists in Rangoon. In 1955, he founded the Bharatiya Bauddha Mahasabha, or the Buddhist Society of India. He completed his final work, *'The Buddha and His Dhamma'*, in 1956. It was published posthumously.

In May 1956, on Buddha's Anniversary, Dr. Ambedkar announced that on October 14, he would embrace Buddhism. When asked, "why"? Dr. Ambedkar replied, "Why can't you ask this question to yourself and... your forefathers...?"

Ambedkar organised a formal public ceremony for himself and his supporters in Nagpur on 14 October 1956. Accepting the 'Three Refuges and Five Precepts' from a Buddhist monk in the traditional manner, Ambedkar completed his own conversion. He then proceeded to convert a large number (some 500,000) of his supporters who were gathered around him. He prescribed the 22 Vows for these converts, after the Three Jewels and Five Precepts. He then traveled to Kathmandu in Nepal to attend the Fourth World Buddhist Conference. His work on *'The Buddha or Karl Marx'* and *'Revolution and counter-revolution in ancient India'* (which was necessary for understanding his book—*The Buddha and His Dhamma*) remained incomplete.

According to Ambedkar, "There is a way of life which has come down as a steady stream in India for thousands of years. Buddhism is not opposed to it. The backward people must rebel against the injustice done to them; they must wipe it out. But 'untouchability' is a problem of the Hindu Society. To solve this, a path that does not harm the culture and the history of India must be followed."

This was the very basis of his resolution to embrace Buddhism.

— *** —

DEATH IN PEACE

Ambedkar had been suffering from diabetes since 1948. He was bed-ridden from June to October in 1954 owing to clinical depression and failing eyesight. He had been increasingly embittered by political issues, which took a toll on his health. His health worsened during 1955. Three days after completing his final manuscript. *'The Buddha and His Dhamma'*. Ambedkar died in his sleep, on December 6, 1956 at his home, in Delhi. He was taken to Bombay after his death.

Since he had converted to Buddhism, a Buddhist-style cremation was organised for him at Dadar Chowpatty beach, Bombay on 7 December, 1956, attended by thousands of people. A conversion program was supposed to be organised on 16 December 1956. So, those who had attended the cremation were also converted to Buddhism at the same place. Since this incidence Dadar Chowpatty is also known as 'Chaitya-Bhoomi'. The Buddhist say, he attained 'Nirvana' here.

Ambedkar was survived by his second wife Dr. Savita Ambedkar (née Dr. Sharda Kabir), who converted to Buddhism with him and later died as a Buddhist in 2002; his son Yashwant (known as Bhaiyasaheb Ambedkar);

and his daughter-in-law Meera Tai Ambedkar. Ambedkar's grandson, who is the national president of the Indian Buddhist Association, Advt Prakash, né Balasaheb Yashwant Ambedkar, leads the Bhartiya Bahujan Mahasangha and has served in both houses of the Indian Parliament.

Dr. B.R. Ambedkar was a lion-hearted man who fought for equality, justice and humanity throughout his life and left etched the same permanently in the form of Indian Constitution.

— ✳✳✳ —

MEMORIES AFTER
HIS DEATH

After his death, a number of unfinished typescripts and handwritten drafts were found among Dr. Ambedkar's notes and papers and were gradually made available. Among these were *'Waiting for a Visa'*, which probably dates from 1935-36 and is an autobiographical work, and *'the Untouchables'*, or *'the Children of India's Ghetto'*, which refers to the census of 1951.

A memorial for Dr. B.R. Ambedkar was established in his Delhi house at 26, Alipur Road. His birthdate is celebrated as a public holiday known as 'Ambedkar Jayanti or 'Bhim Jayanti'. He was posthumously awarded India's highest civilian honour, the Bharat Ratna, in 1990. Many public institutions are named in his honour, such as the Dr. Babasaheb Ambedkar Open University in Hyderabad; Dr. B.R. Ambedkar University in Srikakulam, Andhra Pradesh; Dr. B.R. Ambedkar University, Muzaffarpur, Bihar; the Dr. B. R. Ambedkar National Institute of Technology, Jalandhar; the Dr. Babasaheb Ambedkar International Airport in Nagpur, otherwise known as Sonegaon Airport; Dr. Ambedkar Law University in Tamil Nadu; and the Dr. Ambedkar Government Law College in Chennai, Tamil Nadu. A large official portrait of Ambedkar is on display in the Indian Parliament building.

On the anniversary of his birth (14th April) and death (6th December), and on Dhamma Chakra Pravartan Din (14th October) at least half a million people gather to pay homage to him at his memorial in Mumbai. Thousands of bookshops are set up, and books are sold.

His message to his followers was "Educate! Organize! Agitate!"

This is the message he gave to his untouchable followers years back when they were facing the injustice of untouchability. Today, in India, nobody is an untouchable but the message has the same meaning for all the people of India as they are facing even more acute problems than untouchability. If we chant and put in practice this mantra, most of our social and national problems will be solved.

EXCERPTS FROM
SPEECH & WRITINGS

In 1935 at a conference of Dalits at Yeola, Dr. Ambedker said, "We have not been able to secure the barest of human rights. I am born a Hindu. I couldn't help it, but I solemnly assure you that I will not die a Hindu."

In 1950, on his return from Buddhist conference in Sri Lanka he said in Bombay, "In order to end their hardships, people should embrace Buddhism. I am going to devote the rest of my life to the revival and spread of Buddhism in India."

He wrote in the first issue of *'Mook Nayak'*, "The Hindu society is like a tower of many storeys. It has neither a ladder nor a door to go out... A society which believes the God exists even in inanimate things, also says that many people who are a part of that very society should not be touched."

When Gandhiji sat on a fast unto death against Ambedkar's demand of communal award and separate electorate for depressed class, Ambedkar said, "Muslims, Christian and Sikhs have obtained the right of separate electorate. Gandhiji did not fast to espouse them. Why should Gandhiji fast to oppose Harijans getting separate electorate? If you are unwilling to give the untouchables separate electorate, what other solution is there? It is essential to save Gandhiji but just to save him, I am not prepared to give up the interests of the backward classes. Reserve a larger number of seats for the 'untouchables' than the British have given, then I will give up the claim for separate electorate."

In a debate on Indian constitution he said, "India has lost her freedom only owing to treason of her own people. Raja Dahir of Sindh was defeated by Mohammad Bin Kasim. The only reason for this defeat was that the generals of the Sindh army took bribes from Kasim's men and did not fight for the king. It was Raja Jaichand of India who invited Mohammad Ghori to fight against Prithviraj. When Shivaji was fighting for the freedom of the Hindus, other Maratha leaders and Rajputs were fighting for the Moghals. When the Sikhs were fighting against the British, others did nothing.... Such things should not happen again; therefore, everyone must resolve to fight to the last drop of his blood, to defend the freedom of India".

Regarding his conversion to Buddhism, he said, "I am in the evening of my life. There is an onslaught of ideas on our people from different countries from the four corners of the world. In this flood our people may be confused. There are strong attempts to separate the people struggling hard, from the main life-stream of this country and to attract them towards other countries. This tendency is fast growing. Even some of my colleagues who are disgusted with 'untouchability', poverty and inequality are ready to be washed away by this flood. What about the others? They should not move away from the main stream of the nation's life; and I must show them the way. At the same time, we have to make some changes in the economic and political life. That is why I have decided to follow Buddhism."

He said many times, "God will spare me till I complete my work for the 'Untouchables'!" He lived to see 'untouchability' declared a crime. His entire life was dedicated in securing justice and equality to 'untouchables'.

Ambedkar knew that those who are weak are bound to suffer. He once said, "Goats are sacrificed, not lions."

In his thesis on the origins of untouchability he writes, "The Hindu Civilisation.... is a diabolical contrivance to suppress and enslave humanity. Its proper name would be infamy. What else can be said of a civilisation which has produced a mass of people.... who are treated as an entity beyond human intercourse and whose mere touch is enough to cause pollution?"

While presenting his Draft constitution on November 26, 1949, he said, "I appeal to all Indians to be a nation by discarding castes, which have brought separation in social life and created jealousy and hatred."

He argued for untouchables, "The untouchables are Hindus therefore the doors of temples should be open to them. If the Hindus can touch the Christians and Muslims, why not they touch the people who are themselves Hindus and who have been worshiping Hindu Gods for ages?"

— *** —

MORE ABOUT AMBEDKAR

The two most important qualities that stand out in Ambedkar's life are anger and perseverance. Ambedkar struggled hard to strengthen his people; he knew that those who are weak are bound to suffer. He opposed the British, he opposed the Hindus that were victims of the past, he opposed even Gandhiji, he opposed the Government of free India; he brought justice to the 'untouchables'. At times his own life was in danger; but he gave no heed to it.

He was very learned. At school he was not allowed to study Sanskrit, but later in life he did learn Sanskrit. As the president of the people's Education Society he opened a number of schools and colleges; as a result people of backward classes could get education.

He spent some days in Aurangabad. He saw that there were no plants or trees in the compound of the college. He said that any one who wanted to meet him should plant a sapling; otherwise he (Ambedkar) would not see him. In a few days more than a hundred saplings appeared inside the compound.

The root of his anger was kindness. His heart melted in pity when he saw those who, born as men, lived worse than animals, without the respect and the justice every man should receive. That is why he opposed 'untouchability'.

Once an old lady knocked at his door early in the morning. Weeping, she said, "My husband is very sick. I tried for 12 hours to admit him to the hospital. They said that there was no room in the hospital." He himself went with her and got admitted her husband to the hospital.

Once, a Brahmin boy came to him crying. He was very poor. He had a scholarship for two years. He was doubtful whether he would get it during the last year of his stay. Ambedkar was grieved at his story. He comforted him. He made him sit with him for food. Then he gave him fifty rupees. He patted him on his back and said, "If you are in trouble again, come and tell me."

When he himself was in poor health, he heard that his gardener was not well. He took another man with him and, using a stick for support, went to see the gardener. "Who will look after my wife, if I should die?"— this thought troubled the gardener. He comforted him. He said "Do not cry, everyone has to die one day or the other. I too have to die one day. Be brave. I will send you medicine. You will be all right." He sent the medicine to the poor gardener.

The very next day Ambedkar died in his sleep. It was really brave and kind of him to go for helping a poor gardener while he himself was in such a fragile state of health.

Dr. Ambedkar was born in a cast which was considered as the lowest of the lower. People said that it was a sin it they offered him water to drink, and that if he sat in a cart it would become unclean. But this very man framed the Constitution for the country. His entire life was one of struggles. And his personal life was too miserable; he had lost his first wife and sons. But even then he did not lose his courage. It is no wonder that everyone called him 'Babasaheb', out of love and admiration. Dr. Bhimrao Ambedkar was a lion-hearted man who fought for equality, justice and humanity throughout his life.

— *** —

CHRONOLOGY OF EVENTS

■ Birth of Bhimrao	: 14 April, 1891
■ Passed Matriculation	: 1907
■ Married to Ramabai	: 1907
■ Attained Bachelors of Arts	: 1912
■ Father Passed Away	: 1912
■ Reached USA for Studies	: 1913
■ Attained Doctorate from Columbia University	: 1916
■ Reached London	: 1916
■ Left London and returned to India	: June, 1917
■ The Baroda Episode	: 1917
■ Became Professor at Bombay	: 1918
■ Returned to London for Studies	: 1920
■ Returned to India	: 1923
■ Founded Bahiskrit Hitkarini Sabha	: July 1924
■ The Mahad Sabha	: 19-20 March, 1927
■ The Chavdar Taley Protest	: 25 December, 1927
■ Demand for Seperate Electorate	: 1930-31
■ The Poona Pact	: 24 September, 1932
■ Appointed Principal of Govt. Law College, Mumbai	: 1935
■ Conference at Nasik	: 13 October, 1935
■ Won Bombay Provincial Elections	: 17 February, 1937
■ Won Chavdar Taley case	: 1937

■	Appointed Chairman of Constitution drafting committee	: 29 August, 1947
■	Presented Draft Constitution	: February, 1948
■	Married Dr. Sharda Kabir	: 15 April, 1948
■	Submitted Hindu Code Bill	: October, 1948
■	Draft Constitution adopted	: 26 November, 1949
■	Constitution came into force	: 26 January, 1950
■	Resigned from the Cabinet	: 1951
■	Independently Contested Elections	: 1952
■	Became Rajya Sabha Member	: March, 1952
■	Converted to Buddhism	: 14 October, 1956
■	Expired	: 6 December, 1956

___ *** ___

SOME RARE PHOTOGRAPHS

Dr. Ambedkar with Women delegates of the Scheduled Caste Federation on July 8, 1942 at Nagpur.

Dr. Ambedkar observing Rally of Samata Sainik Dal established at Kamgar Maidan, Parel, Mumbai.

Dr. Ambedkar with his devoted colleagues of the People's Education Society, Bombay. (July 1945)

Members of First Central Cabinet of Indian Republic Dr. Ambedkar at the extreme left of the first row. (Jan.1950)

Dr. Ambedkar addressing the Public meeting held on Buddha Jayanti at New Delhi. The British High Commissioner (sitting) was Chief Guest.

Dr. Ambedkar died on December 6, 1956. The historic (biggest in Bombay History) funeral procession started from Rajgraha on December 7, 1956.